This book started as a joke.
I sent the first of these parables to a friend, and called it a "terrible parable."

I threatened to write a whole book filled with Terrible Parables (or as my friend called them, Tarables).

This book is that book.

Jesus thankfully never told these stories. If you find a bunch of warped theology in these pages, well, that's because I'm not Jesus.

His stories were good.
These stories are awful.

Enjoy.

The kingdom of heaven is like a woman who received a hundred emails. Ninety-nine of them were legit, but one got trapped in the spam folder. So the woman went looking in the spam folder until she found the spammy email and brought it home to her inbox.

The kingdom of heaven is like a Zoom call, where the person who set it up only had the free version, so it could only last for forty minutes. Everybody restarted the call after forty minutes, but one person could not get in. Instead of continuing the meeting, the group called this member's cell phone and walked him through how to get back onto the call.

The kingdom of heaven is like a person who owned a single white shirt. One day his shirt got blood on it, and no amount of laundering the shirt could get the blood stain out. But instead of throwing out the stained shirt, he tye-dyed the shirt. The stained shirt became the most beautiful shirt in his closet.

Partly because it was his only shirt.

But also because it was pretty.

The kingdom of heaven is like a man who thought he saw Bigfoot in the woods. Nobody believed him, and everyone thought he was crazy. But he was persistent and kept looking for Bigfoot, despite the criticism.

The kingdom of heaven is like a person who loses one sock in the dryer, but refuses to see the remaining sock as useless; instead pairing it with another sock that also lost its partner in the dryer.

The kingdom of heaven is like a parent of young kids who wants nothing more than to NEVER WATCH CAILLOU AGAIN, but turns it on anyway because the parent loves the kids and also because the kids will grow up and mature and stop watching it eventually, right? RIGHT???

The kingdom of heaven is like a phone that fell in the toilet, but after sitting in rice for an evening, continued to work for many more years.

The kingdom of heaven is like a comments section with no trolls.

The kingdom of heaven is like the internet with only memes and funny cat videos, and with no vitriol, doxxing, or influencers.

The kingdom of heaven is like a driver who waits for the entire line of ducks to cross the road without honking or revving their engine.

The kingdom of heaven is like a show that might appear to drag on in season 3, but it turns out in season 5 that the entire story arc (the one with the guy who had a mohawk and ate lots of hamburgers and had depressive episodes) that totally seemed insignificant to the rest of the story ended up paying off in huge dividends by the end, and the series ended up having a cult following even larger than The Wire.

The kingdom of heaven is like a group of friends who started a ska band in 2021, knowing that the market for ska music post-1997 was incredibly niche, and also knowing that checkerboard clothing is not, and never was, a good look. Still, they formed the band anyway solely for the love of the music, and they had a long tenure as an affordable wedding band.

The kingdom of heaven is like this:

An awkward 36 year old person did not understand any of the modern lingo that the kids were using in 2020. He still regularly used words like "hip," "fresh," "dope," "rad," and "sick." He felt very old using these words.

But some Very Nice Teenagers had mercy on the Old Man and didn't make fun of his oldness.

Well, not very much anyway.

(this is definitely, positively, not based on my life)

The kingdom of heaven is like a pack of Mentos. Nine out of ten are eaten, but the one Mento left over feels discarded and abandoned. Little does this Mento know that she is destined for greater things. She is carefully placed into a bottle of Diet Coke, and there is a burst of joy not seen anywhere before (except on 192,746,392 YouTube videos).

One tiny Mento brought abounding joy. For two seconds.

The kingdom of heaven is like a Burger King at 7 AM on Black Friday. While most people decided to walk down the Wide Path toward the mall, the few who chose the Narrow Path will enjoy a hearty Croissanwich and a coffee.

The kingdom of heaven is like the kid who started an Instagram account to try and become a famous influencer. He had hopes and dreams, but after 20 days of uploading some boss pictures with sick hashtags and only amassing a follower count of 259, his dreams were shattered. But then a stranger commented on his page, "I'm trying to DM you something but it won't let me. DM me back for details! Make millions of dollars!"

The kid's parents walked in just before he gave his information to the scammer, and was saved from his folly.

I guess the kingdom is more like the parents than the kid.

The kingdom of heaven is like a guy who should have gone to sleep hours ago but still hasn't, because he loves the peace and quiet in his house when everybody else is asleep.

Sure, he'll pay for it tomorrow when he's extremely tired, but coffee can take care of that. Coffee takes care of everything.

The kingdom of heaven is like coffee.

The kingdom of heaven is like this: One day three siblings walked over to the 25 cent candy machines in the front of K-Mart. They begged their mother for a quarter each, and were victorious in receiving said funds. Two of the siblings used their quarters and got some candy. Finally, the oldest sibling placed his quarter in one of the machines and turned the crank. When the crank returned to the default position, the quarter was still there. The eldest son turned the crank again. More candy. The quarter still remained. He brought his two siblings over, and they continued to turn the crank, retrieving more and more candy. They each filled both of their pants pockets with candy, and the eldest son filled his hoodie pocket as well. The machine gave abundantly. All three children ate their fill of candy on the car ride home.

(based on a true story)

The kingdom of heaven is like a man who tried to write some nonsensical parables, and then he tried to write one which was really meta and commented on how ridiculous it is to make up said parables. The whole premise of the Meta Parable was flawed and didn't really work.

The man quickly realized that this was a futile task, as it would never come out as clever or as funny as he had hoped.

This person, in his wisdom, moved on from the Meta Parable, shaking the dust from his feet as he walked away from it.

The kingdom of heaven is like a man who said, "Okay, seriously, I need to go to bed now. It is late, and I have to work in the morning." After a couple more hours, he actually did go to bed, and received the holy and precious abundance of three hours of sleep.

The kingdom of heaven is like a woman who sees the only phone charging station in an airport with dozens of people crowded around. She has a power strip in her bag, and provides increased charging capabilities for all of God's children.

The kingdom of heaven is like a hot tub during a snowy day. When someone first gets in, the heat of the water feels like unwanted acupuncture. However, once the person stays in for a short while, they become accustomed, and it's actually quite pleasant.

The kingdom of heaven is like a kid who took a seed out of the apple he was eating, and planted it in his backyard. He expected that soon, an apple tree would grow and he and his family would have all of the apples that they wanted.

Obviously that was never going to happen.
Still, the kid had hope, and that's something.

The kingdom of heaven is like a kid who enters a rap battle. When the beat drops, she lays down some sick bars, and makes all of the people in the room go "OOOOOOOOOOOOOOOOHHHHHH!" She realizes in that moment that she has found something more than a room full of hip hop fanatics. She has found her people.

The kingdom of heaven is like this:
A man was playing some games with his friends online, but there was a lot of lag, and it made the games borderline unplayable. So the man restarted his live stream to try and fix the problem. The problem was improved, but not entirely fixed. Still, the friends were nice about it and didn't call him mean names or anything, so that was cool.

The kingdom of heaven is like Doctor Strange. He had a movie, and it was okay. Like, Benedict Cumberbatch was good, and everyone did a fine job, but the movie was just okay. It wasn't great, but it wasn't bad. It was just sort of....also there. But for whatever reason, Doctor Strange was able to be one of the most important Avengers in Infinity War and Endgame.

Even though his movie was only okay.

The kingdom of heaven is like Goofy. Goofy is a dog, but he stands up and talks like a human.

He's kind of a dope, but he's also lovable, and he has a good heart.

The kingdom of heaven is also like Pluto. Pluto is a dog, just like Goofy, but he walks around on all fours and barks like a dog.

However, while Pluto does not talk or act like everyone else does, he still gets to be a part of everything.

The kingdom of heaven is **not** like Mickey and Minnie. Mickey and Minnie are Pluto's caretakers. They are friends with Goofy, the walking, talking dog. But they have domesticated Pluto as their pet. People do not domesticate, enslave, or rule over others in the kingdom of God.

The kingdom of heaven is like Pluto. No, not that Pluto. The other Pluto. The ex-planet. Pluto was forced out of the in-crowd just for being different. However, Pluto has never stopped being loved.
Pluto has never stopped existing.
Pluto has never deviated from its mission in life (rotating endlessly), despite the criticism spoken against it.

The kingdom of heaven is like the eight planets that weren't kicked out. They didn't gloat, and they didn't mock when Pluto was dethroned and humiliated. Rather, they continued to do what they were called to do. They continued to rotate endlessly around the solar system.

The kingdom of heaven is like a bag of chips. The chips inside aren't perfectly shaped like Pringles. The bag may not even look too terribly appealing. But the person who buys the chips loves and treasures them.

He treasures them so much he eats the entire bag in one sitting.

The kingdom of heaven is like a party with a terrible DJ. Not just a bad DJ, but a terrible DJ.

The party rules, and everyone's happy to be there, but the DJ's music sucks, and he smells terrible. People would rather he not be at the party at all.

But for whatever reason, once the beat drops, the party goes from "good" to "lit."

Is that what the kids are saying? Lit? Did I use that right?

The kingdom of heaven is like a dude who brings a trombone to a protest. He doesn't have a band, and he doesn't have friends with him.

He comes only with passion and a trombone.

And for whatever reason, it totally works.

The kingdom of heaven is like a goat who thought he was the GOAT. He was arrogant and rude to everyone around him, and nobody would be his friend. But one day, another goat confronted him about his arrogance, and he realized that he was offending the other goats.

He learned that day that trying to be the GOAT might just make you a lonely goat.

The kingdom of heaven is like music. Some of it is awesome, and some of it is crappy children's music that sucks so much it makes you want to remove your ears from the sides of your head.
But that music isn't for you. It's for kids. And they get to enjoy music too.
Music is for everybody.
So is the kingdom.

The kingdom of heaven is like puberty. It makes your voice change, but until you're an adult, this change will cause your voice to crack at inopportune times; like when you're trying to impress a crush, or when you're giving a speech. Still, you always have the hope that one day, you'll have a smooth, sultry voice. Stick with it. Puberty ends eventually. That smooth voice will come.

The kingdom of heaven is like a balloon. To some people, it's just a stupid piece of latex. But to a child, a balloon is the most important thing in the entire world.

No, seriously. Balloons are the most important thing to a child. If you give a 3-year-old a balloon, you instantly earn their love.

A 3-year-old would give up everything he or she has for a balloon.

A 3-year-old would trade his or her family for a balloon.

The kingdom of heaven is like the ozone layer. It's really, really, really, really, really, really, really, REALLY important, and we need it if we want to continue living as a species.

The kingdom of heaven is like the love a five year old has for his Bowser toy. Sure, his dad has stepped on it countless times, and the spikes on Bowser's back hurt worse than a Lego. And yes, his dad wants nothing more than to throw it in the trash while staring his son directly in the eye as he does it. But although his dad will never understand Bowser's value, the five year old knows of Bowser's importance.

The kingdom of heaven is like a person who has endured yet another grueling election year. It beat her up quite a bit, but she is strong, and she made it through. She survived.

The kingdom of heaven doesn't make sense to those on the outside. It is like a kid who asks his parents, "What is 42+78?" The parents have no freaking clue why the kid thought to ask this question. And seriously, it's 6:30 PM and you've been screaming and fighting with your sister all day and we've had to help you with homework and you had a bathroom accident an hour ago and now you want us to DO MATH???!!! Are you freaking kidding me right now???!!! It's not even easy math, either. We're getting into the hundreds here. I have to get out pen and paper now. This is ridiculous.

The kingdom of heaven is like a person who sees that you posted a long lament to your social media, and checks in with you to make sure you're not suicidal. Admittedly it makes you uncomfortable, and even a little angry that they would assume that. However, you also realize the depths of their concern for your well-being, and you remember how rad your friends actually are.

The kingdom of heaven is like coffee. The first time you drink it, it's kind of gross. But as you keep drinking it, the taste grows on you.

The kingdom of heaven is like coffee. You may like a particular kind of coffee more than others. Still, at the end of the day, even though you might have your preferences, if someone hands you a cup of coffee, you're going to drink it. Bad coffee is still coffee.

The kingdom of heaven is like doing a 5,000 piece puzzle. It takes forever, and you feel like giving up much of the time. However, in the end, you recognize that it was worth doing.

The kingdom of heaven is like Charlie Brown's Christmas tree. Sure, it objectively looks like crap, but it's appealing and sentimental in its own way.

The kingdom of heaven is like the song Don't Stop Believin'. No matter how overplayed it may be, if it comes on in a crowded room, everyone gets excited and sings along.

See also: Bohemian Rhapsody and Sweet Home Alabama.

The kingdom of heaven is like using a cloud service. Once you start using a service that autosaves anytime you type a single word, you can never return to something like Microsoft Word.

The kingdom of heaven is like that stupid dinosaur game that comes on when your wifi is down and you try to use Google. Sure, you're sad that you can't use the internet, but hey, at least you can make a dinosaur jump 17,000 times.

It beats doing anything productive with your day.

The kingdom of heaven is like watching a video game speedrun on YouTube. Sure, you may be thinking, "What happened to me? Why am I watching someone else play a videogame?"

But then you realize, "You know what? This may be weird, but I'm having fun." And you keep watching.

The kingdom of heaven is like a computer tech that recovers your important files after your hard drive crashes.

Similarly, the kingdom of heaven is like a mechanic that fixes your car after a crash.

The kingdom of heaven is like watching a slasher movie when you're 12, and realizing that a killer could be in your closet RIGHT NOW.

But then you check, and there's not. And you remember that you're safe.

Mostly.

Unless the killer is in another closet...

(Shout out to Scream for giving me nightmares as a teenager)

The kingdom of heaven is like a kid who won't stop asking her dad to play a game. Even though the dad is exhausted and just wants his kids to shut up and leave him alone, he plays the game because it's important to his kid.

The kingdom of heaven is like a wall that's covered in terrible artwork from a toddler, because the toddler insists on hanging up every single picture that he draws.

Yeah, the pictures are ugly, and yeah, the wall is now hideous, but the pictures remain up.

And the kid is happy.

The kingdom of heaven is like a closed, safe, judgment-free texting group where parents can complain about their kids.

The kingdom of heaven is like a Slinky. There are a bunch of knockoffs, but they just don't work as well as the actual version.

The kingdom of heaven is like pie. It is superior to all other kingdoms, much like pie is superior to all other desserts.

The kingdom of heaven is like creamy peanut butter. It is superior to all other kingdoms, much like creamy peanut butter is superior to crunchy peanut butter.

The kingdom of heaven is like The Last Jedi. It is superior to all other kingdoms, much like The Last Jedi is superior to all other Star Wars movies.

The kingdom of heaven is like a musician who was afraid to release her work into the world, but did it anyway, knowing that it would likely make someone happy.

The kingdom of heaven is like table tennis. It doesn't seem that exciting at first, but when you watch Olympians playing it, you realize that IT'S AMAZING OH MY GOSH WHY HAVEN'T WE BEEN WATCHING THIS BEFORE NOW???

See also: Curling

The kingdom of heaven is like daytime TV soap operas. Somehow or another, they continue to exist. Nothing on this planet seems to be able to make them stop. Not low viewership, not crappy scripts...nothing. They perpetually continue to exist.

Like, my grandma watched them, but does anybody else really?
It's objectively terrible TV.
Who's watching that crap?

The kingdom of heaven is persistent like a kid who won't stop hitting his dad. Like, ever. No, seriously, he's still doing it. He's hitting me currently, while I'm trying to write this sentence. He won't stop. He thinks it's funny.

The kingdom of heaven is like the Oxford Comma. It's important, even if people think it's not.

The kingdom of heaven is like the persistence of a person who scours this book looking for grammatical errors so that they can tell the author about them and make him feel bad.

The kingdom of heaven is like pumpkin pie. It is superior to all other kingdoms, much like pumpkin pie is superior to all other pies.

The kingdom of heaven is like a beekeeper. She knows that bee stings are no fun, but she persists in spite of the danger, and is rewarded with honey.

The kingdom of heaven is like cats. It is superior to all other kingdoms, much like cats are superior to dogs.

The kingdom of heaven is like dog lovers who read that last one and decided not to hate me.

The kingdom of heaven is like new bedsheets.

The kingdom of heaven is like a one year old who found a lollipop on the floor of the Dollar Tree, picked it up, and put it in her mouth before her dad could stop her.

She didn't let the threat of sickness stop her from getting that lollipop.

The kingdom of heaven is like the strength of a father who refused to dry heave in the middle of the store when he watched his one-year-old shove the floor lollipop into her mouth.

Make no mistake, though: he was completely disgusted, and still can't stop thinking about it seven years later.

The kingdom of heaven is like someone who sets his alarm earlier than everyone else in the house, so he can shower first and enjoy all of the hot water.

The kingdom of heaven is like a Christmas tree with a ton of ornaments. The ornaments have no connection to one another, and were added over many years to the ornament stash.

They're kind of weird together.

Spongebob next to Jesus? Ridiculous.

Nevertheless, when all of them are on the tree together, it's absolutely lovely.

The #kingdom of #heaven is like #hashtags. Some #people say that you shouldn't #overuse them, but #forget those #people.

#More #hashtags #equals #more #joy.

The kingdom of heaven is like McDonald's coffee.

It's way cheaper than Starbucks, and it's just as good.

It may even be better.

Fight me.

The kingdom of heaven is like back pain
in your 30's.
It's always there.
It's not going anywhere.
And it's only going to get stronger.

The kingdom of heaven is like Jack. He gave up all of his money for some magic beans.

Jack and the Beanstalk is basically one of Jesus' parables. Think about it: A man sells everything he has for something else.
That's literally what happens in more than one of Jesus' parables.

Jack and the Beanstalk is a parable.

I'll give you a second while you remove your jaw from the floor after that realization.

The kingdom of heaven is like the commitment shown by those dummies who complained in 2015 that Starbucks was trying to kill Christmas because their cups didn't have snowflakes on them.

Yeah, they were being stupid, but they were committed to their cause.

Those people were dumb, though.
Really dumb.
Really, really dumb.

The kingdom of heaven is like a snowball that rolls down a snowy hill and grows larger and larger as it descends.

The kingdom of heaven is like a person who is stressed out by the fact that they have 10,000+ unread emails, so they take a day and a half to do nothing but read and delete emails, fixing their email account while simultaneously healing their soul.

The kingdom of heaven is like a poker player who goes all-in on a hand.

She might seem like she's making a profoundly stupid decision, but she believes in her heart that she has a winning hand.

The kingdom of heaven is like The Cabin in the Woods.

No matter how many times I see it, it's still fantastic. If anything, it only gets better with time.

The kingdom of heaven is like Chuck-E-Cheese. Sure, their pizza is overpriced.
And sure, you're probably not leaving there without getting the flu.
But they have Skee Ball!
Skee Ball is awesome.
So is the kingdom of heaven.

The kingdom of heaven is like a fly who gets inside of your house. It will never find its way out of the house, no matter how many windows you open.

The fly lives with you now.

It has made its home in your home.

The kingdom of heaven is like that movie Deep Impact.

It came out right around the same time that Armageddon did, and they were both about asteroids. But honestly, Deep Impact was the better movie.

By a lot.

Sure, it didn't have the Aerosmith song during the credits, but it didn't need it. It was a better movie with or without Aerosmith.

The kingdom of heaven doesn't need an Aerosmith song to be the best kingdom.

That song is pretty great, though.

"I don't want to close my eyes, I don't want to faaaaalllllll asleep,
Cause I'd miss you baby
and I don't want to miss a thing."

The kingdom of heaven is like ramen. Sure, we all ate a ton of ramen when we were in college, but honestly, it's still great.

Seriously, who doesn't love ramen?

It's a bunch of delicious noodles, cooked in flavored broth.

It's still so good after all these years.

The kingdom of heaven is like Cocoa Krispies. It's great while you're eating it, but it gets even better once you finish the bowl and realize that your milk is now CHOCOLATE MILK!

This first Terrible Parables book was written in 2020, during the Covid pandemic. These last few parables reference the pandemic, and a bit of what it was like to live through it.

The kingdom of heaven is like a streaming service that knows everyone is stuck inside during mandatory quarantine, and offers users a six month free trial.

The kingdom of heaven is like a person who was on ten hours of Zoom calls for work during quarantine, in her attic, wearing sweatpants, while her kids screamed and went nuts downstairs.

Wait...no...the kingdom of heaven is nothing like that. This one was a fail. Abort. Abort.

The kingdom of heaven is like the bathrobe that has hung in the closet for months. But then, suddenly, everybody was given a stay-at-home order, and the 36 year old man-child began to wear the bathrobe everyday. The bathrobe became the most used piece of clothing in the man-child's wardrobe.

The kingdom of heaven is like a music teacher who knows that doing kindergarten via a computer totally sucks, so she offers the students a ton of fun music apps to make the day suck just a little bit less.

The kingdom of heaven is like a guy who found out that Shakespeare wrote King Lear during a plague, and also decided to write a book during a pandemic.

King Lear is quite a bit better than Terrible Parables though...

The kingdom of heaven is like someone who binges the Office and stress-eats every single night just to make it through the pandemic with his sanity, but learns to give himself grace, recognizing that this is a messed up time, and it's probably okay to do some messed up things to cope.

The kingdom of heaven is like an elementary class on Zoom during a pandemic. It's a swirling vortex of chaos, and you can tell that the teacher barely has any sanity remaining, but ultimately you know it's the best thing right now. Zoom school is better than no school.

The kingdom of heaven looks super weird in a lot of ways right now.
None of us have ever lived through a pandemic, and we're all coping and loving and serving in the best possible ways that we know how.

God bless any and all of you who are doing your best.

This book is dedicated to the 2020 pandemic.

I hate you.

However, your existence also caused me to do some profoundly stupid things during the year.

Writing this book is one of those.